Sports Training

Track

Jack Otten

Rigby®

Track
Copyright © 2001 by Rosen Book Works, Inc.

On Deck® Reading Libraries
Published by Rigby
1000 Hart Road
Barrington, IL 60010-2627
www.rigby.com

Book Design: Victoria Johnson
Text: Jack Otten
Photo Credits: Cover, pp. 6–21 by Maura Boruchow; p. 4 (left) © Jonathan Nourok/PhotoEdit; p. 4 (right) © Richard Hutchings/PhotoEdit; p. 5 © Reuters NewMedia Inc./Corbis

Thanks to Chester Upland Middle School Track Team

10 09
10 9 8 7 6

Printed in China

ISBN-13: 978-0-7635-7846-6
ISBN-10: 0-7635-7846-0

Contents

Introduction

Marion Jones is a track star. She is a fast runner. Many young people enjoy taking part in track events.

Getting Started

The Roadrunners meet for track practice. The coach tells the team to warm up. The runners stretch their legs and reach for their toes.

Warming up helps the runners get ready to race.

Runners wear special shoes. The shoes have a lot of soft padding inside of them. They protect the runner's feet.

The coach helps a runner. The runner wants a fast start. She bends down and gets ready to push off.

The coach tells two runners to run around the track.

Practice helps build strong legs. Strong legs help the runners sprint fast.

Relay Races

A relay race is a team event. Each runner on the team runs part of the race. When a runner finishes running, she gives the baton to the next runner.

The next runner holds her hand open. She takes the baton from the runner behind her. This handoff is important.

Step 1

Pass the Baton

Step 2

Take the Baton

Hurdles

The coach helps the runner set up the hurdles.

This hurdle is high. The runner runs and jumps over it.

Running to Win

The coach gets the runners ready to start the race. The runners wait to hear him blow his whistle. Then they push off to get a fast start.

The runners sprint around the track. They run as fast as they can.

The runners cross the finish line.
Each runner leans forward to be
the first to cross the line.

The coach is happy with the team.
They worked hard and practiced well.

Great job!

Glossary

baton (ba-**tahn**) a short rod that is passed from one runner to another in a relay race

handoff (**hand**-awf) when the baton is passed from one runner to the next runner in a relay race

hurdle (**her**-dl) a bar set on posts that runners must jump over while running a race

practice (**prak**-tihs) doing something again and again to learn to do it well

relay race (**ree**-lay **rays**) a four-person race in which each person runs part of the race

sprint (**sprihnt**) to run as fast as possible

track (**trak**) a sport in which people run races

warm up (**worm uhp**) to exercise before playing a sport

Resources

Books

Track and Field
by Donna Bailey
Raintree Steck-Vaughn Publishers, Inc. (1991)

Jesse Owens: Olympic Star
by Pat McKissack
Enslow Publishers, Inc. (1992)

Web Site

Youth Runner magazine
http://www.youthrunner.com

Index